Inquiry into Loneliness

poems by

Meg Harris

Inquiry into Loneliness

Poems ©2017 by Meg Harris
bluemoonnortheast.blogspot.com
all rights reserved by the author

Cover art by the author

Crisis Chronicles #94
ISBN: 978-1-940996-45-5
1st edition, 2nd printing

Published 17 September 2017 by
Crisis Chronicles Press
3431 George Avenue
Parma, Ohio 44134 USA

crisischronicles.com
ccpress.blogspot.com
facebook.com/crisischroniclespress

for my father

Table of Contents

Yariguíes Brush-Finch	1
Origins	2
Inquiry into Loneliness	3
Memory	4
Apnea	5
Paradise Lost	6
Symbiosis	7
Bird Sanctuary	8
Hoboken 2012	9
Vulture	10
For Nonbelievers	11
Sloth	12
Poseidon	14
Travel	15
Vestigial	16
A Rose from Roger	17
Madonna and Child	18
Yes, to Ghosts	19
Starlet	20
Crystal	21
Heartbreaker	23
My Name	24
Acknowledgments	26

Yariguíes Brush-Finch

I tie knots in a blue cord
suck a black pebble
and frieze your name
in a firefly's light

There are graves
speckled with sea salt
and burnt sage
I've exhausted fire
and banishment

Shall I sing backwards
three words three times
run my svelte fingers down
my neck, forgetting
yours?

Naked I smudge
and pray on glowing beads
the waning gibbous on my brow
Venus in my right eye—
a fragile heart beats sound inside
new feather floats down to roots

Origins

Clouded Leopard

To begin it was thought she was bird,
raven, or solitary spotted owl.

Next, her tree dwelling ways,
how she slunk under branches,
lunged headlong down tree trunks.
Of this it was said simply, *squirrel*.

Perhaps not fauna at all, theories grew.
This coat of gray elliptic shadows
and the sorrow provoked
by her poised against the bluest
afternoon sky. Cloud species: alto-cumulus.

Yet hearing of her saber-ic canines,
the gift of balance, her long tail,
and that she'd gone mad in captivity
first killing, then devouring her young,

prowling the corners of her keep,
disappearing entirely and for days,
and how her mate became aggressive
after sexual encounters.

I recognize, but do not declare,
this cousin of mine.

Inquiry into Loneliness

surveying only companions

Robin: Turns a slate tail-feather
upon my approach, flies away.
Diego: Licks between his claws,
bumps his head on the laptop's edge.
Frida: Pounces up—nails in denim, ouch!
Sam: Lies flat, legs extended, head dropped
between paws, stuck to floor like dog-rug,
and then rolls his gaze up woefully.
Dave: After scraping a final forkful of peanut butter
from the plastic jar, dozes off in his chair.
Rock: Says nothing, remaining perfectly still.
Anna: Smiles and nods, *a little bit.*

Memory

II

At about the height of the tree tops,
my flying coach chuckles at me when
I tell her I'd always believed I'd need
actual wings to fly. *Solar plexus,*
Solar plexus, she whispers.

IX

She was too young
when a man took her innocence.
When it was returned to her
it was broken.

LII

Wind-blown curtain,
paint brush, budding forsythia,
whistling tea kettle.
What did I come in here for?

Apnea

This poem is technical yet angelic,
the word apple is in it
and something about the blush of sleep.
This poem is crafty, a petite point.
This poem is a vanity worse than lipstick.
Things are extraordinary.
The moon wanes.
A belly swells.

This poem is structured
in the breathless dream of night
where the sliver-moon sparks magic
and cells are stars dividing—
sailing in the void.

Paradise Lost

The afternoon daisy shivers.
Wander in the fallen leaves.
The wind has winter in its mouth.
The stars are mercury rolling.
Witness the graves,
the children abandoned in paradise.
Sit among the bulrushes and tares,
amidst the star dust,
on the eternal carpet,
weep at the throne of a man.

Symbiosis

A red flower,
disheartened
by the shadow
of a jet, passing
over the sun,
bends to
a motoring
hummingbird.

Bird Sanctuary

Sandpiper, Purple. Passed
away near Coronado's Navy
Seal training camp.
Survived by egg, feathers,
bread-ties, mesh scrubby.
Born in Portland;
Purple's favorites were
blast caps, blue and red.
She enjoyed scavenging.
Remembered for her fear
of birds; her short yellow
legs and Junco-like coloration.
Service September 22nd,
viewing until high tide.

Hoboken 2012

The sun rises with a hiss. In the rain
the objects of your life and the splinters
of your home are bathed into day,
as you slosh in the contaminant of sea

which salts the wound of clutter
that is your home and your neighbor's
home shaken together in a globe of sewage
and gasoline. This the drenched wedding

photo of your parents, sucked now
to glass with a muddied kiss.
You are a seasick captain settled
under this cold and weighty ocean—

the swamp of treasure sunken
and nothing like salvage or salvation.
You want it to recede, to take this new
sandy shore of your decimated living room.

No place to turn for direction, this Titanic
rises and floats away with all the whining
ghosts of what was. It leaves you and others
standing in the reality of nothing.

You, the zygote of the future Hoboken,
this city that could not be washed away.

Vulture

Peace is the dividing cell
ferocious in the marrow.
It coats the bullet,
cannot be marched
to with signs or weapons.
Peace is the vulture
loving the corpse.
It is the victory sign on a mass grave.
It never left, it pulses
under the noise, Peace does.

We thought we could name God.
And we did. All of God's names
are God's names. Even the one
you cannot speak. Peace, too,
has every name we ever gave it.
It is upon the back of the cockroach.
Peace has always loved
the shiny armor of a cockroach.

For Nonbelievers

Your notion of psychosis
acquiesces to my construct of poetry
astonishing spirit flies

Sloth

On April fourth, the prompt was to write a poem about an animal.
I had the idea to write a double sestina about a sloth.

I always felt bad for the sloth; a sin named after it.
Or did they name the animal for the offense?

I thought I'd personalize the poem by tying in my reclusive
tendencies, the chronic depression, my dormant ways.

The sloth keeps an inconstant body temperature—almost reptilian.
My normal body temp is 97.3 degrees. The sloth's known to maintain

a grasp for some fifteen to twenty hours after death. I grind my teeth,
even during afternoon naps, when shoved by a drowse into a cavernous sleep.

The sloth is sedentary enough that a symbiotic alga grows in its fur.
It's not a disinclination to work, I don't think. But that's how Webster

would couch sloth. In the treetops—that's where it all takes place.
The sloth eats, sleeps, and gives birth while hanging from tree branches.

I'd even planned the end words for the sestina: sleep, bough, suspend, hermit, nocturnal and sloth. All month it's made me feel out on a limb

this unwritten poem: sluggish, idle, like I wasn't getting things done.

There are days when stillness, like a death, is the place where I'm suspended.

There, sometimes for hours, I hang.

Poseidon

The stars fly
from your fingertips,
the children
of your netting.
You stoop under
the tender branch
of the sun
as any father might.
Your careful steps
over tree tops
across canyons,
you run the desert
and leap to the
depths of sea.

Travel

I am building a bridge to close
a gulf in the night
rickety boards held up by nothing
more than my steps upon them
when there is no light
I use my other senses
feel me reach for you over
the inky water let the breeze
of my fall from the planet move
your hair walk with me fearlessly
let our faces give the moon a place
to reflect when she is disappearing
as we know she is never gone.
Oh occupation! Lifetime endeavor!
Join me as I travel the un-certainty
of the happy yes of loss.

Vestigial

Heart's a parasitic twin,
calcified from the wounding.
A missing rhythm, hardened
other, the broken love story
between the warrior-girl
hunting the captor of her heart's
imagination and the boy
who loves to run his fingers
the length of her scars.

A Rose from Roger

I have a rose from Roger and Linda loves him.
The cats rendezvous on the rug—I pose

before the rose, before the mirror in dusky candlelight.
My waist is disappearing. A month's worth of daily

news is stacked by the fireplace—I burn it
as sacrament. Dumb words to poems—

smart words to fire—the being inside me tumbles,
the cats murder the garbage—devouring its heart

like fresh kill. I'm strange. I'm wonderful. March
is a wet lion on the lamb—I stand before the lit rose,

the lit mirror, to view pendulous vein-laced breasts,
scary mother-earth tits—the baby counts my ribs.

The Peace Lily blooms. Vacuuming—I recall Roger's
rosebud mouth kissing petals, sipping ambrosia,

as if I were tit and he, babe. Roger saying, *How did that felt?*
Roger saying, *Roger is complicated peoples,* I ask him to say,

Take out the garbage in French and he does. Valentine,
the rose you left presses open in the night glow.

Madonna and Child

A baby's soft skull
Is shaped by its passage
through the narrows of the vagina.
Picture the cone-headed baby Lord,
bald and wailing for his mother's breast.
Where was Jesus better loved
than where he was formed,
in the womb of his mother?

Yes, to Ghosts

Lingering on the shoulder,
candles on gray days,
the green of rain.
Yes, to immortals who love me,
stroke my hair—think they made me.
Yes to divine intervention—
divine anything.

Flying, if only in dreams.
Yes, to the burning effigy
Yes, I say, *yes*.

Starlet

Girl in the nighttime of her attic room—squirrels scratch inside walls and hot cats give infant wails to the summer streets below her darkened window. Under the starlit noise five great hands rise from a floor of clouds. In the center of each hand is a radiant gem. These hands stand, palm to palm, each four times the size of the girl, together they bend open like great lit flower petals. The girl is so young, just a child in her attic bed. Enchanted, she walks the clouded floor. She is a toy ball taken, a soap bubble blown, a blue egg found, beating. Thrust under by the praying hands, under the expanse of shimmering clouds, she floats the breath of infinity, the sac of waters, and vesseled radiance.

Crystal

My mythology is of aliens and angels,
large-eyed, thin-fingered beings
with winged souls, whose light overwhelms.

You dwell with the shadow people
in the new kind of darkness,
with those people whispering in your ear,
but when you look, they disappear.

I am a soap bubble, thin-skinned and full of wind,
an ocean of rainbows floats upon me.
Yet, I am almost nothing.

You've married madness, a toothless wench
full of riddles. *This is the last time.*
She murmurs this promise over and over.

I sleep in a veil of sensuous dreams
and dwell in the garden.

You rock in a cradle of nightmares
and sleep in the desert.

The whole world went bad for you,
under the homeless bridge,
up from the battered dumpster,
You swallow the seed of despair.

Crystal transforms you and me.
I cup my hands under the rainbow
it throws on the floor, straining to lift it
for Abigail. I drop it again and again,
to the delight of her waiting toes.

You draw the bad stuff into your lungs
and all of your colors come to darkness.

Heartbreaker

Janis went into hiding
her hair cut in a bob.
She wore pumps
and cleaned up—good.

Janis went down
to the basement laundry.
She married a salesman who
didn't feel the way she felt.

It didn't matter—much.
Janis hid behind a baby-belly.
She smoked in secret
and screamed at her cry-baby

kids running-on-the-lawn.
Janis lived in hiding. She went
to cocktail parties. Her manicure
looked natural, her perfume spiced the air.

She baked a clam dip.
She worried about her weight.
Channeling Janis; no one sees my drunken
bounce off the walls of her psyche.

They don't hear her moan into the needle
at the edge of identity. I'm a mother, a housewife.
I'm Janis. Laundry—dive into the sheets of night.
Dust—cough into a tragic cigarette.
Breakfast—drowse in the shattered invisible—
detach and linger—in the rafters.

Did I make you feel?

My Name

This is my name. Now quiet. This is. This is. Quiet now. Quiet now. Quiet now. My name is yours. I give you my name. My name is under my toenail. It is between my teeth. My name is mother-woman and I am larger than my name. My name is power. It is all the power of the unseen. It is all the power of void. My name is Isis. No. Inanna. No. Gwan Yin. No. Patricia. No. Julia. No. My name is unspeakable. Can you hear it above the cough? the bark? the water flow? My name is nothing and I am so much more than empty. I am more than missing. I am larger than black hole. My name is not yet and I am still waiting in the fluid sac. My name is missing. Who took it? Who took my name?

Acknowledgments

Yariguíes Brush-Finch	The Café Review
Inquiry into Loneliness	The Barefoot Review
The Trouble with Babydoll	The Barefoot Review
Sloth	The Barefoot Review
Vulture	The Café Review
Poseidon	Vox Poetica Unbound Content
Paradise Lost	The Café Review

Also, some of my poems appear on my blog: www.bluemoonnortheast.blogspot.com.

Thanks for this wee book: First to my friend, editor and publisher John Burroughs of Crisis Chronicles Press who believed in these poems and wanted to see them in print. To my children who inspire art in me, always. To my best friend, love, and fellow traveler Dave Kibler who makes all things possible, worthwhile, and joyful. And finally, to all women writers who dare to say. You are my steam.

— Meg Harris

www.ingramcontent.com/pod-product-compliance
Lightning Source LLC
Chambersburg PA
CBHW060227050426
42446CB00013B/3199